OXFORD BOOKWORMS LIBRARY
Playscripts

The Murder of Mary Jones

Stage 1 (400 headwords)

Playscripts Series Editor: Clare West

TIM VICARY

The Murder
of
Mary Jones

OXFORD UNIVERSITY PRESS

OXFORD

UNIVERSITY PRESS

Great Clarendon Street, Oxford OX2 6DP

Oxford University Press is a department of the University of Oxford.
It furthers the University's objective of excellence in research, scholarship,
and education by publishing worldwide in

Oxford New York

Auckland Cape Town Dar es Salaam Hong Kong Karachi
Kuala Lumpur Madrid Melbourne Mexico City Nairobi
New Delhi Shanghai Taipei Toronto

With offices in

Argentina Austria Brazil Chile Czech Republic France Greece
Guatemala Hungary Italy Japan Poland Portugal Singapore
South Korea Switzerland Thailand Turkey Ukraine Vietnam

OXFORD and OXFORD ENGLISH are registered trade marks of
Oxford University Press in the UK and in certain other countries

ISBN 978 0 19 423502 0

A complete recording of this Bookworms edition of
The Murder of Mary Jones is available on audio CD ISBN 978 0 19 423508 2

Printed in Hong Kong

Illustrated by: Kevin Lyles

For more information on the Oxford Bookworms Library,
visit www.oup.com/elt/bookworms

CONTENTS

INTRODUCTION

This is a court in England. The people in the court are trying to answer a question – did Simon Clark and Dan Smith kill Mary Jones, or not? It is a very important question, because in Britain, murderers usually go to prison for life. You can see a picture of the court on page 2. Simon and Dan are there, with two policemen, the judge, the clerk of the court, two lawyers, and the twelve people in the jury. Witnesses come to the witness box, and the lawyers and the judge ask them questions. The jury do not say anything, but they listen carefully. At the end, they must answer the question – are Simon and Dan guilty of murder, or not guilty?

There are two possible endings to the play, Scene 4 (Alternative 1) and Scene 4 (Alternative 2). Read and discuss them, and decide which you like best.

PERFORMANCE NOTES

Scenes 1 to 4: The courtroom

At the back of the room is the judge's table and chair. In front of this there is a chair and table for the clerk of the court. On the left of the judge's table is a chair for the witnesses (the witness box). In front of the clerk's table is a table with two chairs for the lawyers. Behind this table there are four more chairs for Simon, Dan, and two policemen. On the judge's left there are twelve chairs for the jury. There are more chairs in the room for people to sit and watch.

CHARACTERS IN THE PLAY

The judge
The clerk of the court
Ms Helen Wills, the police lawyer
Simon Clark, a young man
Dan Smith, a young man, Simon's friend
Mr David Carter, Simon's and Dan's lawyer
Jim Wilson, Mary Jones's boyfriend
PC Norton, a policeman
Dr Seldon, a doctor
PC Moran, a policeman
WPC Gray, a policewoman
Mrs Lucy Symes
Janet Nolan, a young woman
Mrs Jones, Mary's mother
The jury (twelve people)

The Murder of Mary Jones

How did Mary die?

*The jury, the lawyers, and the clerk of the court come in
and sit down. Then Simon Clark and Dan Smith come
in with the two policemen. The judge comes in and
everyone stands up. The judge walks to his chair, looks
at everybody slowly, and then sits down. The people
and the lawyers sit down. Simon and Dan, the two
policemen, and the clerk are standing up.*

CLERK   Simon Clark, you are here because of the murder
of Mary Jones. Did you kill her, or not?

SIMON   No, sir. I didn't.

CLERK   And you, Dan Smith? Did you kill Mary Jones?

DAN   No, sir. I didn't. I'm not guilty!

SIMON   We didn't kill her!

CLERK   All right. Sit down. (*They sit.*)

MS WILLS   (Standing up) My lord, I am Helen Wills, the
lawyer for the police. David Carter is the lawyer
for Simon Clark and Dan Smith.

JUDGE   Very good. Please begin, Ms Wills.

MS WILLS   Thank you, my lord. Members of the jury, look

1

The courtroom.

at the photo, please. There is a girl in the photo with a young man. She is Mary Jones, and he is Jim Wilson, Mary's boyfriend. (*The jury look at the photo.*)

JUDGE   Ms Wills, I haven't got that photo.

CLERK   Oh, I'm sorry, my lord. Here you are.

He gives the judge a photo.

JUDGE   Thank you. Please go on, Ms Wills.

MS WILLS   On 12 August, Mary was in a disco in Trenton with Jim. At midnight, she started to walk home along the road by the sea, and someone killed her. Now, please look at the second photo.

JUDGE   Excuse me, Ms Wills. (*He holds up a photo.*) This photo? The photo of a dead girl?

MS WILLS   Yes, my lord, that's right. I'm sorry, it isn't a very nice photo. But that is Mary Jones, too. There is blood on her head and face.

JUDGE   Yes, I see. Did someone find her there, that night?

MS WILLS   Yes, my lord. Jim Wilson found her body on the beach near the road at about half past twelve. He tried to help her, but he couldn't. Mary Jones was dead.

JUDGE   How did she die, Ms Wills?

MS WILLS   She died because someone hit her four times on the head with a spanner, my lord. Clerk, can I have the spanner, please?

CLERK   Yes, here you are. (*He gives her a spanner.*)

MS WILLS   Thank you. It was this spanner, members of the jury. Look at it carefully. This spanner has Mary's blood and hair on it. Can you see that? *She shows the spanner to the jury.*

JUDGE   Can I see that, please, Ms Wills?

MS WILLS   Yes, of course, my lord. (*She gives it to him.*)

JUDGE   Thank you. But who hit her with the spanner, Ms Wills? That's the important question, you know. Who killed her?

MS WILLS   Who killed her? It was Simon Clark and Dan Smith, I think.

JUDGE   Why do you think that? Tell the jury, please.

MS WILLS   Yes, my lord. They were in the disco that evening. They went there in a car, a white Ford Fiesta. It wasn't their car – they stole it. They often steal cars.

JUDGE   I see. And how long were they there?

MS WILLS   They were in the disco for two hours. At about ten o'clock, Dan danced with Mary Jones. After that,

'This spanner has Mary's blood and hair on it.'

4

Simon Clark danced with her.

JUDGE Excuse me, Ms Wills. Did Jim see this?

MS WILLS Yes, my lord, he did. He was very angry, and he hit Simon. Then he talked to Mary for half an hour, and after that Mary started to walk home alone.

JUDGE And Jim stayed in the disco?

MS WILLS Yes, my lord, he did. But Dan and Simon didn't. They went out, ten minutes after Mary. They drove away in the Fiesta.

JUDGE Yes. But did anyone *see* them kill her? That's important.

MS WILLS No, no one saw them kill her. But the police found the tyre marks of a Ford Fiesta near Mary's body. And later, they found Dan and Simon in a white Ford Fiesta in Bilsford.

JUDGE Where is Bilsford, Ms Wills?

MS WILLS Ten kilometres from Trenton, my lord. And in the car there was a spanner. This spanner, members of the jury! With Mary's blood and hair on it! (*She shows the spanner to the jury.*)

JUDGE I see. That's very important. (*He writes.*)

MS WILLS Yes, my lord. These two boys followed Mary from the disco in the white Fiesta. They stopped the car, hit her on the head with this spanner, and drove away.

5

DAN   (*Standing up*) It's not true! We didn't follow her! We didn't go down that road! It's not true!

JUDGE   Be quiet, young man! Sit down! You can talk later!

MS WILLS   I call my first witness, PC Norton.

        PC Norton goes to the witness box.

CLERK   (*Giving him a book*) Take this book in your right hand and read what it says.

NORTON   I promise to tell the truth, the whole truth and nothing but the truth.

MS WILLS   PC Norton, what happened on 12 August?

NORTON   Well, at 12.47 a.m. someone telephoned the police and I went to the road by the beach in Trenton. I found a young woman's body there, and a young man. His name was Jim Wilson.

MS WILLS   I see. Did Jim call the police?

NORTON   Yes, he did. He was Mary's boyfriend, I think. He tried to help her, but she was dead.

MS WILLS   Where was the body?

NORTON   It was on the beach near the road. There were some tyre marks in the sand near the body. A car stopped there, and then went back towards Trenton, I think.

MS WILLS   Thank you. Wait there, please, and answer Mr Carter's questions. (*She sits.*)

CARTER   (*Standing up*) PC Norton, tell me some more

'Jim sat in my car and started to cry.'

about this boyfriend, Jim Wilson. He tried to help
the dead girl, you say. Did he have blood on his
shirt and trousers?

NORTON Yes, sir, he did. There was blood on his face and
hands and on his shirt and trousers too.

CARTER Did you ask him about this?

NORTON Yes, sir. The blood was there because he tried to
help her, he said. He sat in my car and started to
cry. He loved her, he said.

CARTER I see. But why was Jim on the beach?

NORTON He went for a walk after the disco, he said.

CARTER I see. Thank you very much. (*He sits down.*)

JUDGE PC Norton, one more question. Were there any
cuts on Jim's face or hands?

NORTON I don't know, sir. There was blood on his face and hands, but it was Mary Jones's blood, I think.

JUDGE Thank you. That's all. The next witness is Dr Seldon, I think. (*Dr Seldon comes in, and the clerk gives him the book.*)

SELDON I promise to tell the truth, the whole truth, and nothing but the truth.

MS WILLS Dr Seldon, you looked at Mary Jones's body. What did you find?

SELDON Mary Jones was a young woman of about 18. She died because somebody hit her four times on the head.

MS WILLS Thank you. You looked at this spanner very carefully, too. Can you tell us about that, please?

SELDON Yes. I looked at the spanner and I found blood and hair on it. The blood and hair were Mary Jones's.

MS WILLS Are you sure about that?

SELDON Yes. They were the same.

MS WILLS So did somebody kill her with this spanner?

SELDON Oh yes. I am sure about that.

MS WILLS Thank you. Wait there, please.

Ms Wills sits down, and Carter gets up.

CARTER Dr Seldon, I want to ask you about Mary Jones's hands. Was there any blood on them?

SELDON Yes, sir, a lot of blood. I looked at it very

carefully and it was her blood. Perhaps she put her hands on her head when the spanner hit her.

CARTER But was there blood under her fingernails, too?

SELDON Yes, a little.

CARTER Did you look carefully at that blood, too?

SELDON No, I didn't. There was a lot of blood on her hands and it was all her blood. I am sure about that.

CARTER Yes, but think carefully, doctor. What did Mary do when the man hit her? Did she try to hit him, too? Perhaps she cut his face with her fingernails. Do girls sometimes do that?

SELDON Well, yes, sometimes.

CARTER So perhaps the man's blood was under her fingernails. Did you look for that?

SELDON There wasn't much blood under her fingernails.

CARTER But did you *look* at it, doctor? Did you look carefully at the blood under her fingernails?

SELDON No. I'm sorry, I didn't.

CARTER I see. But there *was* some blood

'A little blood under her fingernails.'

under her fingernails. You're sure about that?

SELDON Yes, there was a little blood there. Not much.

Carter sits down. Seldon goes out. PC Moran comes in, and takes the book from the clerk.

MORAN I promise to tell the truth, the whole truth, and nothing but the truth.

MS WILLS PC Moran, you looked at the white Ford Fiesta, I think. What did you find?

MORAN Well, first I put some paper under each tyre, and drove the car over it. The tyres made marks on the paper. Then I took the paper to the beach, and looked at the tyre marks in the sand.

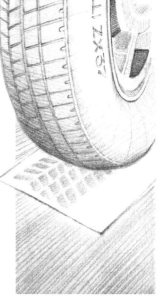

MS WILLS Were they different?

MORAN No, they weren't. The marks on the beach were from Pirelli ZX37 tyres, and the marks on the paper were from Pirelli ZX37 tyres, too.

'I put some paper under each tyre, and drove the car over it.'

MS WILLS Did you find any more things in the car?

MORAN Yes. There was a lot of sand from the beach.

MS WILLS I see. That's very interesting. Thank you very much. Wait there, please. (*She sits down.*)

CARTER (*Standing up*) PC Moran, do all Ford Fiestas have Pirelli ZX37 tyres?

MORAN No. Ford Fiestas can have lots of different tyres.

CARTER And what about Volkswagen Polos? Do they sometimes have Pirelli ZX37 tyres, too?

MORAN Sometimes, yes, sir.

CARTER I see. So there are lots of cars with these tyres. Some are Ford Fiestas, but some are Volkswagen Polos. Is that true?

MORAN That's true, yes.

CARTER So perhaps a Polo made these marks in the sand?

MORAN Perhaps, yes.

CARTER Thank you. Now, there was a lot of sand in the car. Was there any blood in the car too, or hair?

MORAN No, there wasn't.

CARTER What? No hair or blood? Did you look?

MORAN Yes, sir, we did. But we didn't find anything.

CARTER But Ms Wills said, 'These young men killed Mary Jones.' There was blood on Mary's head and face, blood on her dress, blood on her hands. But there was no blood in the car, you say?

MORAN   No, sir, no blood or hair in the car.

CARTER   I see. Thank you, PC Moran. That's very
interesting. *(He sits down.)*
Moran goes out, and WPC Gray comes in.

GRAY   *(Taking the book)* I promise to tell the truth, the
whole truth, and nothing but the truth.

MS WILLS   WPC Gray, you found Simon Clark and Dan
Smith in the white Ford Fiesta. What happened?

GRAY   Well, at ten o'clock that night, a woman called
Mrs Symes telephoned the police. 'I can't find my
car,' she said. It was a white Ford Fiesta, number
M346 WXT.

MS WILLS   Did you look
for the car?

GRAY   Yes. At two
o'clock in the
morning, we
found it in
Bilsford. Simon
Clark and Dan
Smith were in
the car, so we
asked them a lot
of questions.

MS WILLS   What did they
say?

'We asked them a lot
of questions.'

12

GRAY   They stole the car at eight o'clock, they said. Then they went to a disco in Trenton, and stayed there until about midnight.

MS WILLS And what did you find in the car?

GRAY   A spanner, and a lot of sand. There was sand in the young men's shoes, too.

MS WILLS What did they say about the spanner?

GRAY   Nothing. They said, 'Spanner? What spanner?'

MS WILLS Why was there sand in their shoes? Did you ask them?

GRAY   Yes. They went for a walk on the beach, they said.

MS WILLS Did you see any blood on these young men?

GRAY   Yes, I did. There was blood on Simon Clark's face. He had two small cuts under his left eye.

MS WILLS Did you ask him about this?

GRAY   Yes. He said, 'A man in a disco hit me. His hand cut me.'

MS WILLS I see. Thank you very much. Wait there, please. (*She sits down, and Carter stands up.*)

CARTER I have only two questions, WPC Gray. Did you find any blood on the young men's shoes?

GRAY   No, sir. There was a lot of sand, but no blood.

CARTER Was there any blood on their shirts or trousers? Blood from these cuts on Simon's face, perhaps?

GRAY   No sir, there wasn't. They were very small cuts.

CARTER Thank you. (*He sits down.*)

Jim's story

Jim Wilson goes to the witness box.

CLERK *(Giving Jim the book)* Take this book in your right hand and read from it.

JIM I promise to tell the truth, the whole truth, and nothing but the truth.

MS WILLS *(Standing up)* Jim, tell me about Mary. Did you know her well?

JIM Very well. She was my girlfriend. Our families come to Trenton for a holiday at the same time every year.

MS WILLS I see. Can you tell us about the night of Saturday 12 August, please?

JIM Well, I went to the disco with Mary at half past eight. We sat at a table and talked to our friends. Then we danced – talked – danced – and then Mary went home.

MS WILLS What time did she go home?

JIM At about – midnight, I think. I don't remember.

MS WILLS Did you see any new people at the disco?

JIM Yes. Two young men. They danced with Mary.

MS WILLS Can you see those two young men here now?

JIM Yes. Those two there. They killed her! (*He looks*

'They killed her!'

angrily at Simon Clark and Dan Smith.)

DAN   (*Standing*) We didn't kill her! That's not true!

JUDGE   Please, Mr Smith. Sit down!

Dan sits down slowly.

MS WILLS I'm sorry about that. Now Jim, tell me, what
did you do when Mary went out of the disco?

JIM   Well, I stayed for fifteen minutes, to talk to some
friends. Then I went for a walk, and – I saw her.
There was blood on her face. I tried to help her,
but I couldn't.

MS WILLS So what did you do then?

15

JIM   I ran to phone the police. But it was no good. She was dead – and they killed her!
He looks at Dan and Simon. Ms Wills sits down.

CARTER   (*Standing up*) Jim, did you love Mary?

JIM   Yes, I think so – she was my girlfriend.

CARTER   Yes, she was your girlfriend. And you loved her – you think. Mary left the disco at midnight, you say. She walked along that dark road by the sea. You didn't go with her. Why?

JIM   Why? I don't know – she wanted to go alone.

CARTER   Why? Was she angry with you?

JIM   I don't know. A little angry, perhaps. It wasn't important.

CARTER   Were you angry with these young men? With Simon and Dan, because they danced with her?

JIM   A little angry, yes.

CARTER   A little angry, you say. Did you see them dance with her?

JIM   I saw Simon dance with her, but not Dan. I went out with some friends. They wanted to see my car.

CARTER   To see your car? Why? Is it very interesting?

JIM   It's a new car – a Volkswagen Polo. I like it very much. My friends wanted to look at it.

CARTER   I see. What happened when you went back in?

JIM   I saw Mary with that boy. (*He looks at Simon.*)

CARTER   And what did you do then?

'I was angry, so I hit him.'

JIM   I was angry. I asked him to stop dancing with her.

CARTER   You *asked* him, you say. Did you hit him, Jim?

JIM   Well, yes. I hit him once. But he hit me first!

SIMON   That's not true! I didn't hit you! *You* hit *me*!

JUDGE   Be quiet, Mr Clark! Please!

SIMON   But it's not true, my lord! I didn't hit him!

JUDGE   Perhaps not. But you can speak later. Do you understand?

SIMON   Yes, sir.

CARTER   What did Mary do when you hit Simon, Jim?

JIM   She laughed, I think. Then she sat at a table with me.

CARTER   Why did she laugh, Jim? Did she laugh at Simon, or you?

JIM   She laughed at Simon, because he was afraid of me!

CARTER   Is that true? Or did she laugh at you, Jim? Perhaps she liked Simon, not you!

JIM   Of course she didn't! She was *my* girl, and she was there with *me*, not them!

CARTER   But you were angry with Mary, Jim. Why was that? Did she like them more than you, perhaps?

JIM   NO! I wasn't angry with *her*, I was angry with Simon!

CARTER   Are you sure?

JIM   Yes, of course! I was angry with him because he danced with my girlfriend, and because he killed her. Don't you understand? *He killed her*! Of course I'm angry – *he killed her*!

CARTER   How do you know that, Jim?

JIM   Everyone knows that! He followed her in his car along the road. Then he took that spanner from the car, and he hit her on the head – two, three times! Then she ran on to the beach, crying.

'He hit her on the head.'

CARTER What happened then, Jim?

JIM He hit her again! And then she stopped moving, and there was blood everywhere! Lots of blood! And I tried to help her, but I couldn't, she was dead –
Jim is crying. Carter says nothing for a minute.

CARTER So, Jim, she ran on to the beach, crying, and he hit her again, you say. How do you know that?

JIM How? I don't remember. The police said that.

CARTER No, Jim, they didn't say that. (*He waits, but Jim says nothing.*) Jim, there was no blood on Simon or Dan, but there was a lot of blood on *you*. And you were angry with Mary, because she didn't love you. Is that true, Jim?

JIM No.

CARTER Simon and Dan weren't on the beach, Jim. They didn't kill her. But *you* were there. You went out of the disco and followed her. Did *you* kill her?

JIM NO! Of course I didn't! What are you saying? *They* killed her – *their* car was there, the spanner was in *their* car! I didn't kill her! She was my girlfriend – I *loved* her!

CARTER You loved her, you say. But you didn't walk home with her on that dark night, Jim. Why not?

JIM But I did! I went after her! And I found her on the beach! She was dead!

CARTER Did you go in your car? Your new Polo?

JIM   No, I didn't. I walked. I wanted to think.

CARTER   What did you want to think about?

JIM   About me and Mary. I was sorry – I loved her, you
         know – And I wanted to talk to her, of course. But
         she was dead! They killed her, she was dead!

CARTER   But there was no blood on them, or in their car,
         Jim. The blood was on *you*! Perhaps you loved
         Mary, but you killed her too – because you were
         angry with her!

JIM   No! Of course I didn't! I didn't kill her. I loved her!

CARTER   One more question, Jim. Do you have Pirelli tyres
         on your Volkswagen Polo?

JIM   What? Er – no. No, I don't. I have Goodyear tyres.

CARTER   All right. I have no more questions. *(He sits.) Jim
         goes out, and Ms Wills stands up.*

MS WILLS My lord, I have no more witnesses.

JUDGE   Thank you. Mr Carter, have you any witnesses?

CARTER   Yes, my lord. Mrs Lucy Symes, please.
         Lucy Symes comes into the witness box.

SYMES   *(Taking the book)* I promise to tell the truth, the
         whole truth, and nothing but the truth.

CARTER   Mrs Symes, do you have a white Ford Fiesta?

SYMES   Yes, sir.

CARTER   What is the car's number?

SYMES   M346 WXT.

CARTER   And what happened to that car on 12 August?

SYMES   Somebody stole it, sir. I telephoned the police, and they found it next day. There was a lot of sand in it.

CARTER   I see. Now, Mrs Symes, do you have a spanner in your car, like this spanner on the table?

'*I telephoned the police.*'

SYMES   Well, I don't know, sir. You see, I did have a spanner like that in the car last year, but it wasn't very good. So now I have a better one than that.

CARTER   I see. And where is this new spanner now?

SYMES   In the back of my car, sir. It's always there.

CARTER   What about the old spanner? Where is that?

SYMES   Well, I don't know, sir. I didn't want it, you see.

CARTER   Was it in the car on 12 August?

SYMES   I don't know. Perhaps it was, but I'm not sure.

CARTER   Thank you, Mrs Symes. Please wait there.

He sits down, and Ms Wills stands up.

21

MS WILLS Mrs Symes, was your old spanner in the car, or not?

SYMES I'm not sure. I'm sorry, I don't know.

MS WILLS Well, perhaps you put the spanner in the back of your car, and then you forgot about it.

SYMES Yes, perhaps I did.

MS WILLS Yes. (*She takes the spanner from the table and gives it to Mrs Symes.*) And is this spanner like your *old* car spanner?

SYMES I think so, yes. Yes, it is.

MS WILLS Thank you. (*She sits down.*)

Mrs Symes leaves. Janet Nolan comes to the witness box, and takes the book from the clerk.

JANET I promise to tell the truth, the whole truth, and nothing but the truth.

CARTER Miss Nolan, you were in the disco on the night of 12 August. Did you see Mary Jones?

JANET Yes, I saw her with her boyfriend, Jim. And then later she danced with those two boys.

CARTER Which two boys?

JANET Those two. (*She looks at Simon and Dan.*)

CARTER I see. Did she dance with them for a long time?

JANET For about ten minutes, yes. She danced with Dan first and then Simon. Jim wasn't in the disco then. When Jim saw them, he was very angry.

CARTER What did he do?

'*Mary danced with Dan first and then Simon.*'

JANET   He hit Simon.

CARTER   And what did Simon do?

JANET   Nothing. He didn't hit Jim. He walked away.

CARTER   I see. And was Jim angry with Mary, too?

JANET   Yes. Mary laughed at Jim, so Jim was very angry.

CARTER   Mary laughed at Jim, you say? Not at Simon?

JANET   Yes, that's right.

CARTER   What happened then?

JANET   Well, Jim and Mary talked, then Mary went home.

CARTER   I see. And what did Jim do?

JANET   He sat there for five minutes. Then he went out.

CARTER   What about Simon and Dan? Where were they?

JANET   They stayed in the disco. One of them asked me to dance, but I said no. So after ten minutes he and his friend went out.

CARTER   Now I want to be sure about this. Jim went out first, you say, and these boys went out ten minutes *after* him. Is that right?

JANET   Er, ye–es, I think so. It's not easy to remember.

CARTER   Thank you.

   He sits down and Ms Wills gets up.

MS WILLS   You're right, Miss Nolan. It isn't easy to remember things after six months, of course.

JANET   No, it isn't. But I can remember nearly everything.

MS WILLS   Did you watch Mary and Jim all the time in the disco?

JANET   No, of course not. But—

MS WILLS   No. So be careful, Miss Nolan. Perhaps you are wrong about this. It's a long time ago. Perhaps these boys went out *before* Jim? Not *after* him?

JANET   Perhaps. I don't know. I'm not sure.

MS WILLS   Thank you. That's all.

   She sits down. Janet begins to go out of the witness box, then she stops.

JANET   No, I'm right! Jim *did* go out first – I'm sure!

JUDGE   Thank you, Miss Nolan. Thank you very much.

24

Simon and Dan tell their story

Simon Clark comes into the witness box.

SIMON   *(Taking the book)* I promise to tell the truth, the whole truth, and nothing but the truth.

CARTER   Now, Simon. This is very important. What happened on the night of 12 August? Tell me.

SIMON   All right. Well, I went out with Dan to look for a car. We often take cars, you see—

JUDGE   You steal them, do you?

SIMON   Not *steal*, no. We take them for the night, drive for an hour or two, and leave them somewhere.

JUDGE   I see. Do you do this often?

'We often take cars.'

25

SIMON   Yeah, why not? We like it. That night we took
        this white Ford Fiesta, and went to the disco in
        Trenton. We got there about ten o'clock, I think.

CARTER Did you meet anyone in the disco?

SIMON   Yes. We danced with some girls. But it wasn't
        very exciting, so at about midnight we went out
        and drove away. Two hours later a police car
        stopped us. That's it.

CARTER Now I want you to look at this photo of Mary
        Jones. Did you see her in the disco?

SIMON   Yes. Dan danced with her first, and then I
        danced with her. Then her boyfriend hit me.

CARTER Did you hit him first?

SIMON   No, I didn't.

CARTER Did you hit him after he hit you?

SIMON   No. He was bigger than me. And I never hit
        people.

CARTER All right. Did you follow this girl out of the
        disco?

SIMON   No, I didn't see her go out. Dan and I talked for
        ten minutes, then we drove away. We didn't see
        the girl.

CARTER Did you kill her?

SIMON   No, sir, I didn't.

CARTER All right. (*He sits down. Ms Wills stands up.*)

MS WILLS   When Jim hit you, you did nothing. Right?

SIMON   Yes. That's right.

MS WILLS   And what did Mary do? Did she laugh?

SIMON   I'm not sure. Perhaps she did.

MS WILLS   She did, I think. Mary was a beautiful girl, and
        she laughed because her boyfriend hit you.

SIMON   I wasn't angry. She wasn't important to me.

MS WILLS   Not important? But you danced with her.

SIMON   She was OK. She wasn't very beautiful or
        interesting.

        Mary's mother stands up. She is very angry.

MRS JONES   Don't you say that about my daughter! She
        was beautiful, and she was a lot better than you!
        She didn't steal cars or kill people!

JUDGE   Please sit down, Mrs Jones. (*She sits down.*)

'Don't you say that about my daughter!'

MS WILLS You weren't angry, you say. That isn't true,
Simon Clark. You were *very* angry with Mary!

SIMON No, I wasn't. Why do you say that?

MS WILLS You were angry with her because she laughed
at you. So you and Dan followed her in the
Fiesta. What happened then? You asked her to
get in. *Did* she get in?

SIMON No, she didn't.

MS WILLS I see. She didn't get in the car, so you were

angry again. Then you
hit her with this
spanner and killed her.
Is that right?

SIMON No. It's not true.

MS WILLS Yes, it is. You
murdered Mary Jones,
Simon Clark! You
killed her with this
spanner!

SIMON No, I didn't! I'm
not guilty, I tell you!

MS WILLS You *are* guilty,
Simon. You killed Mary
Jones.

*'I promise to tell the truth,
the whole truth, and nothing
but the truth.'*

*She sits down. Simon
goes out. Dan comes in.*

28

DAN   *(Taking the book)* I promise to tell the truth, the whole truth, and nothing but the truth.

CARTER   Dan, you listened to Simon. Did he tell the truth?

DAN   Yes, of course he did.

CARTER   Did you see Jim hit your friend in the disco?

DAN   Yes, I did.

CARTER   And after that, did you see Jim go out?

DAN   Yes. The girl, Mary, went out first. Jim went later. We stayed, and went out ten minutes after Jim.

CARTER   And when you went out, did you see Jim or Mary?

DAN   No. We got in the car and drove away.

CARTER   All right, thank you. Wait there.

        He sits down, and Ms Wills stands up.

MS WILLS   When Jim hit Simon, did Mary laugh at him?

DAN   Well, yes.

MS WILLS   Mary laughed at Simon?

DAN   Yes.

MS WILLS   So then Simon was angry with Mary, but you were both afraid of Jim. Is that right?

DAN   Well, perhaps, yes.

MS WILLS   Yes. So you waited in the disco. You were angry with Mary. She went out of the disco, and Jim wasn't with her. So you and Simon followed her in the car.

DAN   No, we didn't.

MS WILLS Oh yes, you did. You stopped the car, and asked her to get in. But she didn't. Perhaps she laughed at you again. Then you were really angry.

DAN NO! That's not true!

MS WILLS Oh yes it is, Dan. How did Mary die? I know, and the jury know too. You killed her. But I'm not sure about one thing – who hit Mary first? Was it Simon?

DAN No—

MS WILLS It wasn't Simon, you say? Then it was you!

DAN No, it wasn't! It wasn't me!

MS WILLS So it was Simon?

DAN No! It wasn't Simon or me! *We didn't do it!*

MS WILLS Do you see this spanner, Dan? It has Mary's blood on it, and Mary's hair. And this spanner was in your car. Tell me, Dan – who put it there? You, or Simon?

DAN I don't know. I didn't put it there. I didn't see it.

MS WILLS That isn't true, Dan. The spanner was in your car because you murdered Mary Jones with it. That's true, and everybody knows it.
She sits down. Dan goes out of the witness box. Carter stands up.

CARTER I have no more witnesses, my lord. (*Sits down.*)

JUDGE Now, members of the jury, Ms Wills and Mr Carter are going to talk to you. Listen carefully.

'Members of the jury . . .'

MS WILLS (*Standing up*) Members of the jury, the police found this spanner in the Fiesta. It had Mary's blood and hair on it. They found tyre marks near Mary's body. There was blood on Simon's face, and under Mary's fingernails, too.

SIMON Jim hit me in the disco! He cut my face!

JUDGE Be quiet! Ms Wills is talking now, not you!

MS WILLS Look at these two young men. They're angry now. Think about them. They aren't very nice young men. What do they do in the evenings? They steal cars.

DAN Yes, but we don't kill people!

MS WILLS You did, this time. You followed Mary, and you killed her. Think about it carefully, members of the jury. Mary is dead, and these young men are guilty of her murder.

She sits down, and Carter stands up.

MRS JONES *(Standing up)* That's right. They killed my
         beautiful daughter!

JUDGE   Please, Mrs Jones. You must sit down. Mr
         Carter is going to talk now. (*She sits down.*)

CARTER Members of the jury, Mary Jones is dead, we
         know that. But did these two boys murder her?
         Are you sure about that? There are a lot of
         questions to answer.

MRS JONES What questions? They're guilty! We know that!

JUDGE   Mrs Jones, you must sit down, or go out!
         She sits down.

CARTER Think about Janet Nolan. She says, '*Jim* went
         out of the disco first – not Simon.' Think about
         the spanner. Did it come from Mrs Symes's car?
         Perhaps, perhaps not.

JIM   What about the tyre marks? The Fiesta had
         Pirelli tyres!

CARTER Hundreds of cars have Pirelli tyres, Jim.
         Volkswagen Polos have them. And you have a
         Polo, Jim.

JIM   But my car doesn't have Pirelli tyres!

CARTER Perhaps your car doesn't have Pirelli tyres *today*,
         Jim. But in August? Did you have Pirelli tyres
         then?

JIM   No, of course I didn't.

'There was a lot of blood on your shirt and trousers, Jim.'

CARTER   Well, you say that now. But I'm not sure. And here's another question – what about the blood? There was a lot of blood on your shirt and trousers, Jim.

JIM   Of course there was. I tried to help Mary!

CARTER   But was there any blood on Simon or Dan? No, members of the jury, there wasn't.

JIM   There was blood on Simon's face!

CARTER   Yes, but you hit him, Jim. There was no blood on Dan, or in the car. There was blood on you. And you're a big young man, Jim – you get angry very quickly. Mary was afraid of you.

JIM   That's not true! I loved her!

CARTER   Yes, Jim, but you were angry with her too. And you are angry now, we can see that.

JIM   I'm angry because Mary is dead, and they killed her!

33

'Are they guilty or not guilty?'

CARTER   Did they, Jim? I'm not sure. Think carefully, members of the jury. Did Jim kill Mary? Perhaps – we don't know. But did Simon and Dan kill her? No. They are not guilty. (*Carter sits down.*)

JUDGE   Now, members of the jury, there is one big question for you, and you must answer it. Think very carefully. Did these two men kill Mary Jones? Are they guilty or not guilty of her murder?

The Verdict (Alternative 1)

The judge, the lawyers, the clerk of the court, and Simon and Dan are all in their places. There are two policemen beside Simon and Dan. The jury come back into the room and sit down. The foreman of the jury stands up. The clerk stands up.

CLERK Members of the jury, do you have a verdict?

FOREMAN Yes, we have.

CLERK And what is your verdict? Guilty, or not guilty?

FOREMAN Guilty.

DAN No! No, that's not true. We didn't do it!

CLERK Be quiet! Simon Clark and Dan Smith, stand up, please!

They stand. Dan looks at Simon.

DAN What did I tell you, Simon? Why did we go to that disco? Why did you want to follow that girl?

SIMON I didn't! Be quiet!

JUDGE Simon Clark and Dan Smith, you murdered Mary Jones – a young, beautiful girl. For this murder, there is only one punishment. You must go to prison for life.

DAN But we didn't do it! Jim killed her, we didn't!

JIM No, I didn't! I loved her! You murdered her!

35

'You murdered her, we didn't!'

SIMON   That's not true! *You* murdered her, we didn't!

JUDGE   Be quiet. Take them away, please.

The police take Simon and Dan out. Mrs Jones stands up.

MRS JONES   Members of the jury, my lord judge, Ms Wills, thank you. Thank you very much.

JUDGE   That's all right, Mrs Jones. I'm very sorry about Mary, but those boys are going to prison now.

JIM   (*Takes Mrs Jones's arm.*) Yes. Come on, Mrs Jones. It's all right now. (*They go out of the court.*)

The Verdict (Alternative 2)

*The judge, the lawyers, the clerk of the court, and
Simon and Dan are all in their places. There are two
policemen beside Simon and Dan. The jury come back
into the room and sit down. The foreman of the jury
stands up. The clerk stands up.*

CLERK   Members of the jury, do you have a verdict?

FOREMAN   Yes, we have.

CLERK   And what is your verdict? Guilty, or not guilty?

FOREMAN   Not guilty.

DAN   Yes!

SIMON   That's right! That's right! We didn't do it!

CLERK   Simon Clark and Dan Smith, stand up, please.
        Simon and Dan stand up. Dan looks at the jury.

DAN   (*Happily*) Thank you, jury! Thank you very much!

JUDGE   Simon Clark and Dan Smith, you are not guilty
        of the murder of Mary Jones. You are free to go.

MRS JONES   But they killed my daughter! They can't be
        free!

JUDGE   I'm sorry, Mrs Jones, but they are not guilty.

SIMON   What about Jim? What are you going to do
        about Jim? He killed her!

JIM   I'm going home now.

*He walks to the door. PC Norton walks in front
of him. He puts his hand on Jim's arm.*

NORTON   Jim Wilson, come with me. I want to talk to
you about your girlfriend, Mary Jones.

JIM   But she's dead. Those two boys killed her!

NORTON   No they didn't. They're not guilty. Come with
me, please. (*Jim and the policeman go out.*)

DAN   Come on, Simon. We're free! We're going home.
They go out. Mrs Jones looks at the judge.

MRS JONES   My lord, my daughter is dead. Who killed her?

JUDGE   I'm sorry, Mrs Jones. I don't know.
*The judge looks at Ms Wills and Mr Carter.
They say nothing. Slowly, Mrs Jones goes out.*

'Jim Wilson, come with me.'

GLOSSARY

alone not with any other people
beach a sandy place near the sea
boyfriend, girlfriend a special friend for a girl or boy
cut (*n*) a break in the skin, where blood comes out
cut (past tense **cut**) to break the skin with something sharp
dance to move your arms and legs when you listen to music
disco a place to listen to music, meet people and dance
follow to go behind someone
foreman the person who speaks for the jury
guilty someone who has done something wrong
lawyer a person who knows about the law
murder to kill someone, not by accident
my lord a polite way of speaking to a judge
prison a place where bad people are locked up
punishment sending people to prison is a punishment
sand usually yellow or white, found on a beach
show to help someone to see something
sir a polite way to speak to a man who is more important
than you
steal (past tense **stole**) to take things that belong to other people
story telling about something that happened
sure feeling that you know something very well
try (past tense **tried**) to attempt something or see if you can do
something
verdict what a jury decides at the end of the court case
witness someone who sees something happen

I promise to tell the truth, the whole truth, and nothing but the truth
what every witness must say in court, so that we know they are
going to tell the truth

The Murder of Mary Jones

ACTIVITIES

Before Reading

1 **Read the information on the first page of the book and the back cover, then circle the correct words.**

   1 In a British murder trial, *lawyers / the jury / the police* ask most of the questions.
   2 The trial happens in a *prison / courtroom / police station.*
   3 In Britain, a person who is guilty of murder must *die / pay a lot of money / go to prison.*

2 **Which of these people are usually in court?**

   ambulance driver, doctor, footballer, judge, jury, lawyer, police, student, taxi driver, teacher, witness

3 **Read the back cover. How much do you know now about the people in the play? Match the people with the information.**

   Jim / Mary / Simon / Mrs Jones / Dan

   1 _____ is dead.
   2 _____ had blood on his face.
   3 _____ was Mary's boyfriend.
   4 _____ and _____ had the murder weapon in their car.
   5 _____ wants to know who killed her daughter.

While Reading

Read Scene 1. Choose the best question-word for these questions, and then answer them.

What / Where / Who / Why

1 . . . was Mary on 12 August in the evening?
2 . . . went to the disco with Mary?
3 At the disco, . . . was Jim angry?
4 . . . was Mary at midnight?
5 . . . found Mary's body?
6 . . . did someone use to kill Mary?
7 . . . did the police see on the sand near the body?
8 . . . stole Mrs Symes's car?

Read Scene 2. Who said these words in this scene?

1 'I tried to help her, but I couldn't.'
2 'And you loved her – you think.'
3 'I didn't hit you. *You* hit *me*!'
4 'I telephoned the police, and they found it next day.'
5 'Mary laughed at Jim, so Jim was very angry.'
6 'Perhaps you are wrong about this. It's a long time ago.'

Here are some untrue sentences about Scenes 1 and 2.
Change them into true sentences.

1 Helen Wills is the lawyer for Simon and Dan.
2 Mary left the disco with Jim.
3 Somebody hit Mary once on the head.
4 Simon had two small cuts on his leg.
5 Jim's family goes to Brighton every year.
6 Jim's new car is a Fiesta.

Read Scene 3. Simon is talking about the night of the
murder. Use these words to complete the sentences.

*bigger, drove, exciting, friend, hit, midnight, never, often,
stopped, took, Trenton, white*

I went out with my _____ Dan. We _____ a car. We _____
take cars. It was a _____ Ford Fiesta. We _____ to a disco
in _____. I danced with a girl, and her boyfriend _____ me.
I didn't do anything – he was _____ than me. And I _____
hit people. The disco wasn't very _____, and we left at
about _____. Later, the police _____ us.

What do you think now about the murder? Who was the
killer? Do you think it was . . .

1 Jim?   2 Simon and Dan?   3 a different person?

Before you read Scene 4, can you remember what these words mean? Match the words with their meanings.

foreman

jury

verdict

punishment

lawyers

twelve people in court who decide if someone is guilty or not

making people pay, or sending them to prison, for what they have done

people who know a lot about the law

the person who speaks for the jury

what the jury decides: guilty or not guilty

Read Scene 4 (Alternative 1). Complete these sentences. (Use as many words as you like.)

1 The _____ asks the jury for their _____.

2 The _____ finds Simon and Dan _____.

3 The judge sends Simon and Dan _____.

4 Dan is _____ with Simon.

5 Mrs Jones says thank you to _____.

Read Scene 4 (Alternative 2), then answer these questions.

1 The verdict is 'not guilty'. Why, do you think?

2 How do Simon and Dan feel when they hear the verdict?

3 How does Mrs Jones feel?

4 What is going to happen to Jim?

5 Why does the judge say 'sorry' to Mrs Jones?

After Reading

1 **Match these people with the sentences. Then choose the best ending for each sentence, and complete it with the correct linking word.**

Mary / Mrs Symes / Simon / Jim / Mrs Jones

1 _____ phoned the police . . .
2 _____ and his friend took a car . . .
3 _____ started to walk home from the disco . . .
4 _____ is angry with Simon and Dan . . .
5 _____'s spanner wasn't very good . . .

and / because / but / so / when

6 _____ drove it to Trenton.
7 _____ she thinks they killed her daughter.
8 _____ she bought a new one.
9 _____ he found Mary's body on the beach.
10 _____ she never arrived at her house.

2 **What did Jim say to Mary before she left the disco (see page 17)? Put their conversation in the right order, and write in the speakers' names. Jim speaks first (number 6).**

1 _____ 'What? Are you going to hit me, just like you hit Simon? I've had enough of you. I'm going!'

2 _____ 'You know what I mean. I saw you dancing with those two boys!'

3 _____ 'Come here! Where are you going?'

4 _____ 'Haha! You always think about yourself, don't you!'

5 _____ 'What's wrong with that? I can dance with other boys if I want to!'

6 _____ 'You must never do that again! Do you understand?'

7 _____ 'No, you can't! You're my girl. You're with me, not them.'

8 _____ 'I'm going home. I want to be alone. I don't want to be with you any more!'

9 _____ 'What do you mean? I haven't done anything wrong!'

10 _____ 'Don't laugh at me! If you laugh at me again, I'm going to . . .'

3 **Write a short review of the play. Use these words to help you.**

I like / don't like this play because _____ .

It is a good play because _____ .

My favourite character is _____ because _____ .

I prefer ending 1 / 2 because _____ .

4 Find fifteen words from the play hidden in this word search, and draw lines through them. The words go from left to right, and from top to bottom.

I	W	F	I	E	S	T	A	A	S	A	N	G
R	D	R	I	V	E	Y	Y	W	H	A	N	D
I	T	H	W	H	I	R	C	L	E	R	K	M
B	E	F	I	N	G	E	R	N	A	I	L	S
C	A	U	T	S	E	V	E	R	D	I	C	T
S	P	A	N	N	E	R	H	J	U	D	G	E
F	A	C	E	E	D	O	A	U	N	C	E	D
W	I	T	S	H	M	A	Y	R	H	A	I	R
G	I	R	S	L	F	D	R	Y	I	E	N	D

Put the words into these three groups:

Courtroom: *judge*, _____ _____ _____ _____

Cars: *tyre*, _____ _____ _____ _____

Parts of the body: *face*, _____ _____ _____ _____

5 Look at the word search again and write down all the letters that don't have a line through them. Begin with the first line and go across each line to the end. Can you find a sentence of eleven words?

1 What is the sentence?
2 Who said it?
3 Who is the speaker talking about?

6 **A week after the trial, Mrs Symes is talking to a friend about the case. Fill in the gaps with these words from the play.**

blood, court, drove, found, killed, morning, questions, remember, sand, sell, stole

'I was in _____ last week! Someone _____ my car – do you remember? Well, the police _____ it. Two boys took it and _____ it to Trenton. Later, at two o'clock in the _____, a police car stopped them. There was a lot of _____ in the car. My old spanner was in the car, too – and there was _____ on it! Somebody _____ poor Mary Jones with it! In court, they asked me a lot of _____ about the spanner, but I couldn't _____ very much. I don't want to use the car again. I'm going to _____ it and buy a new one!'

7 **How did Mary Jones die? These are two possible explanations. Which one do you think is true? Why?**

1 Simon and Dan left the disco and followed Mary in the Fiesta. They were angry with her. One of the boys took the spanner from the back of the car and hit her with it. Then they drove away.

2 While Simon and Dan were still in the disco, Jim went into the car park. He took the spanner from the Fiesta. He ran after Mary and killed her with it. Then he came back to the car park, put the spanner in the Fiesta, and drove to the beach in his Polo.

49

ABOUT THE AUTHOR

Tim Vicary is an experienced teacher and writer, and has written several stories for the Oxford Bookworms Library. Many of these are in the Thriller & Adventure series, such as *White Death* (at Stage 1), or in the True Stories series, like *The Coldest Place on Earth* and *The Elephant Man* (also at Stage 1).

Tim Vicary has two children, and keeps dogs, cats, and horses. He lives in York, and works at the University of York, in the north of England. He has published two long novels, *The Blood upon the Rose* and *Cat and Mouse*, and also a crime novel, *A Game of Proof*, under the name of Megan Stark.

OXFORD BOOKWORMS LIBRARY

Classics • Crime & Mystery • Factfiles • Fantasy & Horror
Human Interest • Playscripts • Thriller & Adventure
True Stories • World Stories

The OXFORD BOOKWORMS LIBRARY provides enjoyable reading in English, with a wide range of classic and modern fiction, non-fiction, and plays. It includes original and adapted texts in seven carefully graded language stages, which take learners from beginner to advanced level. An overview is given on the next pages.

All Stage 1 titles are available as audio recordings, as well as over eighty other titles from Starter to Stage 6. All Starters and many titles at Stages 1 to 4 are specially recommended for younger learners. Every Bookworm is illustrated, and Starters and Factfiles have full-colour illustrations.

The OXFORD BOOKWORMS LIBRARY also offers extensive support. Each book contains an introduction to the story, notes about the author, a glossary, and activities. Additional resources include tests and worksheets, and answers for these and for the activities in the books. There is advice on running a class library, using audio recordings, and the many ways of using Oxford Bookworms in reading programmes. Resource materials are available on the website <www.oup.com/elt/bookworms>.

The *Oxford Bookworms Collection* is a series for advanced learners. It consists of volumes of short stories by well-known authors, both classic and modern. Texts are not abridged or adapted in any way, but carefully selected to be accessible to the advanced student.

———————————————

You can find details and a full list of titles in the *Oxford Bookworms Library Catalogue* and *Oxford English Language Teaching Catalogues*, and on the website <www.oup.com/elt/bookworms>.

THE OXFORD BOOKWORMS LIBRARY
GRADING AND SAMPLE EXTRACTS

STARTER • 250 HEADWORDS

present simple – present continuous – imperative –
can/cannot, must – going to (future) – simple gerunds …

Her phone is ringing – but where is it?

Sally gets out of bed and looks in her bag. No phone. She looks under the bed. No phone. Then she looks behind the door. There is her phone. Sally picks up her phone and answers it. ***Sally's Phone***

STAGE 1 • 400 HEADWORDS

… past simple – coordination with and, but, or –
subordination with before, after, when, because, so …

I knew him in Persia. He was a famous builder and I worked with him there. For a time I was his friend, but not for long. When he came to Paris, I came after him – I wanted to watch him. He was a very clever, very dangerous man. ***The Phantom of the Opera***

STAGE 2 • 700 HEADWORDS

… present perfect – will (future) – (don't) have to, must not, could –
comparison of adjectives – simple if clauses – past continuous –
tag questions – ask/tell + infinitive …

While I was writing these words in my diary, I decided what to do. I must try to escape. I shall try to get down the wall outside. The window is high above the ground, but I have to try. I shall take some of the gold with me – if I escape, perhaps it will be helpful later. ***Dracula***

... should, may – present perfect continuous – *used to* – past perfect –
causative – relative clauses – indirect statements ...

Of course, it was most important that no one should see
Colin, Mary, or Dickon entering the secret garden. So Colin
gave orders to the gardeners that they must all keep away
from that part of the garden in future. ***The Secret Garden***

STAGE 4 • 1400 HEADWORDS

... past perfect continuous – passive (simple forms) –
would conditional clauses – indirect questions –
relatives with *where/when* – gerunds after prepositions/phrases ...

I was glad. Now Hyde could not show his face to the world
again. If he did, every honest man in London would be proud
to report him to the police. ***Dr Jekyll and Mr Hyde***

STAGE 5 • 1800 HEADWORDS

... future continuous – future perfect –
passive (modals, continuous forms) –
would have conditional clauses – modals + perfect infinitive ...

If he had spoken Estella's name, I would have hit him. I was so
angry with him, and so depressed about my future, that I could
not eat the breakfast. Instead I went straight to the old house.
Great Expectations

STAGE 6 • 2500 HEADWORDS

... passive (infinitives, gerunds) – advanced modal meanings –
clauses of concession, condition

When I stepped up to the piano, I was confident. It was as if I
knew that the prodigy side of me really did exist. And when I
started to play, I was so caught up in how lovely I looked that
I didn't worry how I would sound. ***The Joy Luck Club***

Much Ado About Nothing

WILLIAM SHAKESPEARE

Retold by Alistair McCallum

There are two love stories in this fast-moving comedy.

Brave young Claudio and Leonato's pretty daughter Hero are in love and want to marry, but Don John has a wicked plan to stop their wedding. Will he succeed, or will the truth come out? Will Claudio and Hero marry, after all?

Beatrice and Benedick are always arguing with each other, but how do they really feel? Perhaps they are more interested in each other than they seem to be! Their friends work hard to bring them closer together.

One Thousand Dollars and Other Plays

O. HENRY

Retold by John Escott

Money or love? Which is more important in life? Can money buy anything? Can it help a young man to marry the girl he loves? Does money really make people happy, or does it just cause problems?

We all know how difficult love can be. When you meet someone you like, there are so many things that can go wrong, sometimes because you are trying too hard, sometimes because of a misunderstanding.

These four plays about money, love and life are adapted from short stories written a hundred years ago by the great American storyteller O. Henry. Henry had his own difficulties with money and loneliness, and wrote from personal experience.